OUR TRIUNE GOD

Living the Mystery!

William O. Scherzer, III

Print ISBN 978-1-66784-010-9

Book layout and design, including images and graphics, by William O. Scherzer, III

All scriptures were copied online from King James, New International and Holman versions of the Bible.

OUR TRIUNE GOD - Living the Mystery! is self published utilizing the tools, resources and printing services of:

BookBaby Book Printing and Self Publishing Services

7905 N. Crescent Blvd. Pennsauken, NJ 08110

www.bookbaby.com

www.OurTriuneGod.com

INTRODUCTION

God is a mystery - as He should be. We will ultimately solve the mystery when we arrive in heaven. Investigating a mystery reveals truths that drive us to descovery. YOUR discovery starts now!

I had a pastor that, during one of his sermons, made the statement "Try to understand the Trinity, you could lose your mind. To deny the Trinity, you could lose your soul." In context, the pastor was pointing out that the mystery of the Trinity is well beyond the common logic and spiritual teaching that most people receive in our churches.

I was pricked by the Spirit at the time and did not realize it. I had a concept of the Trinity that I was at peace with and was bothered that other people were struggling with it. I was able to share with a few people I was around and helped them, but it was years before I matured enough for God to direct me in presenting the concept to classes and study groups - and ultimately in writing this book. (Also, my concept has expanded well beyond what I had at the time.)

Two thoughts I have heard over the years may direct perspective:
> "An infinite God cannot be fully described by our finite understanding."
>
> "What kind of God would He be if He could be understood and explained by us?"

Mentally, our minds cannot fully comprehend what we do not have the ability to visualize. However, we can use revelation from God via the resources that have been given to us to enlighten us.

The mystery of God: Father, Son and Holy Spirit: three persons – one God – three in one – truly our Triune God! Understanding the fact inside this mystery and living in conjunction with our Triune God will take your "walk with God" to a whole new level.

Listen to the Holy Spirit.

In studying the Trinity, I found the more I learned, the more there is for me to learn. I realized that God – our triune God – affects all aspects of our life. In this book, I share the understanding I have – that every area of our Christian life is affected by fact that God is the Trinity.

As I matured in spiritual growth and sought how to present the Trinity so others would see our awesome God as I do, the more I read the Bible and the more I understood that the Holy Spirit is the key. The best source of understanding our Triune God is the Holy Spirit and the Bible which He inspired men to write. His purpose for being with us is to help us understand.

In your quest for understanding the Trinity, seek the Holy Spirit's guidance and wisdom.

Romans 11:

33 Oh, the depth of the riches both of the wisdom and knowledge of God! How unsearchable are His judgments and His ways past finding out!

34 "For who has known the mind of the Lord? Or who has become His counselor?"

1 Corinthians 2:

6 We do, however, speak a message of wisdom among the mature, but not the wisdom of this age or of the rulers of this age, who are coming to nothing.

7 No, we declare God's wisdom, a mystery that has been hidden and that God destined for our glory before time began.

8 None of the rulers of this age understood it, for if they had, they would not have crucified the Lord of glory.

9 However, as it is written: "What no eye has seen, what no ear has heard, and what no human mind has conceived - these things God has prepared for those who love him"

10 for God has revealed them to us by his Spirit. The Spirit searches all things, even the deep things of God.

11 For who knows a person's thoughts except that person's own spirit within? In the same way no one knows the thoughts of God except the Spirit of God.

12 We have not received the spirit of the world but the Spirit who is from God, that we may understand what God has freely given us.

13 This is what we speak, not in words taught us by human wisdom but in words taught by the Spirit, explaining spiritual realities with Spirit-taught words.

14 The person without the Spirit does not accept the things that come from the Spirit of God but considers them

foolishness, and cannot understand them because they are discerned only through the Spirit.

15 The person with the Spirit makes judgments about all things, but such a person is not subject to merely human judgments,

John 16:

13 When the Spirit of truth comes, he will guide you into all the truth, for he will not speak on his own authority, but whatever he hears he will speak, and he will declare to you the things that are to come.

14 He will glorify me, for he will take what is mine and declare it to you.

We are reborn as we accept Jesus' death on the cross and are even called babies:

1 Corinthians 3:1-3

And I, brethren, could not speak to you as to spiritual people but as to carnal, as to babes in Christ. I fed you with milk and not with solid food; for until now you were not able to receive it, ...

A baby starts with milk and is given meat as they are able to digest it. As a baby grows we teach them more and more "details" of what we know. We don't go into details of a combustion engine until they can grasp the concepts. We just let them see us turn the key and the car starts and works.

As babies in Christ, the truths of the Bible are revealed the same way. (Unfortunately too many people stay babies.) As we mature, the Holy Spirit reveals new things to us as we are able to use what we learn.

To understand this mystery of God, do not proceed without asking the Holy Spirit to reveal the truths that you should receive from the perspectives presented in this book.

Contents

WHAT IS THE TRINITY?

Throughout the Bible, this "mystery" of God is revealed. From the beginning, Satan has tried to keep it hidden - and he is a master of deception. Our understanding of the Trinity gives us power over Satan, so he lies and deceives to keep this knowledge from us.

Human Concepts

I have heard different ways that people explain the Trinity:

1) One person - three hats > a family man is father, son and husband. The idea is that God is a single entity and depending on how you look at Him determines His description.

2) One element - three forms > H2O is water, ice and steam. The idea is that God is a single element that manifests in the three forms that we know as Father, Son and Spirit.

3) One entity - three persons > Father, Son and Spirit. The idea is that God is three individuals (per our limited understanding) working together in unity as the entity we know as "God"

I have no problem with either 2) or 3). The main problem I have with 1) is all the times Jesus prayed to the Father. If they are the same person, wouldn't Jesus talking to Himself all the time be awkward?

He taught His disciples to pray "Our Father which is in heaven" while He was standing right there with them. That would seem odd if they are the same being.

Also, in Genesis 1:26, God said "Let "us" make man in "our" image"; then in verse 27 it says God created man. Question: Who is the "us" that created man? Sure sounds like the work of a triune God to me.

(I cover this in detail in the chapter "Three Persons?")

We won't know for sure until we get to heaven; but for the purpose of this book, I am focusing on the Bible's awesome depiction of the inner-workings of the three entities we have come to know as the Father, the Son and the Holy Spirit – aka. the Trinity.

Concept of what I call "singular plurality"

I define this as a singular word that by its definition acknowledges a unity of multiple parts.

When you hear or see words like family, team, company, audience, army, etc.; your mind automatically acknowledges that multiple persons are united to create that singular unit. Each word expresses a single entity and is described as such (A family, THE team, AN audience …), yet each is a plurality in composure and is thus a "singular plurality".

Our government: A "singular plurality" and an example of a trinity.

The word "government" is used in a singular sense ("the" government). Everyone readily knows that it is plurality depicting thousands of people working as one unit.

Our government is also a trinity – three independent branches, united, working as one. There are three entities that form "the" government – legislative branch, executive branch and judicial branch.

"Each" branch is of itself a "singular plurality" as the single branch is made up of many people / departments; however, all three branches are just one government. All three branches have specific and separate functions and not one individually is the totality of government.

The legislative branch makes the laws, the executive branch executes the laws and the judicial branch decides right and wrong based on the laws made by the legislative branch. No individual branch is "government" by itself. All three branches united is government – thus it is a trinity.

When we speak of government, we refer to the combined work of all three branches; however, government is also credited for the work of each individual branch.

For example: "Our government sent troops to Iraq." Most people acknowledge that statement; however, it is not technically correct. The president (as leader of the executive branch) sent our troops. He did receive the blessings of the legislature later, but the judicial branch did not have anything to do with it. Just the same, "government" as a whole is acknowledged for the action.

Another example I've often heard: "Trying to raise taxes again! That's our government for you." Here "government" is getting tagged for what the legislative branch was doing.

The point is, any time you hear the word "government", if you think about it, you will see that most of the time only one or two of the branches is really at work.

Another example: "The Marines took the island." Actually, it would be a division, a platoon, a squad, … some unit or another (all singular pluralities also), but not all Marines – yet the Marines as a whole get credit.

"God" is a singular plurality and trinity

Our word "God" is a singular plurality – a singular word that describes the unit of three parts. (I see this as one of the "mysteries" of the Bible that Satan is trying to keep hidden.)

"God" IS the Trinity (tri-unity - three united – three in one). We even sing it in church, "God in three persons – Blessed Trinity".

One God > the Father, the Son, the Holy Spirit > the Trinity.

Old Testament revelation of the Trinity

Though the "Father/Son/Spirit" concept was not available in the Old Testament, the Bible was actually written with the full revelation of the plurality of God.

The Hebrew word "Elohim" (used 2602 times in the Old Testament and translated to the singular word "God" in all but a few places – ie "other gods") is the plural of "El" or "Eloah". It was no mistake, or typo, for them to use a plural word so many times when the singular word was available. I see it as a revelation of "fact".

The plural words "adoni" and "adonai" is translated as the singular word "Lord" over 450 times in the Old Testament. The word "adon" is the singular form for "lord". Our "Lord" is translated from "adoni" and "adonai".

The following verses accentuate the incredible use of "Elohim" and "Adonai" as singular pluralities when referencing our "God" and our "Lord".

Genesis 1:
26 "Then God (Elohim) said (singular verb), 'Let us make (plural verb) man in our image, after our likeness'".

The plural word "Elohim" is supported by singular verbiage.

Exodus 20:
3 "Thou shalt have no other gods (elohim) before me."

This shows that the Hebrews also used the word "elohim" when referring to multiple gods. Their use of the plural "Elohim" for our singular "God" was not just an oversight.

Psalms 77:

13 "Your ways, God (Elohim), are holy. What god (el) is as great as our God (Elohim)?"

The Hebrews used "el" to describe the single-person god to contrast our multi-person God.

Dueteronomy 6:

4 Listen, Israel: The LORD our God, the Lord is One.

The Hebrew is precise in verse 4: The Lord (Yah-weh) our God (Elohim), the Lord (Yah-weh) is One. Moses came as close as any I have found in the Bible trying to reveal the plurality of our single God.

We can see the Trinity at work – especially in Isaiah. All throughout the book of Isaiah, "God" and "Lord" are used primarily in reference to works of the Son and "Lord God" is primarily used when referring to works of the Father. This can most clearly be seen in Isaiah 48:12-16:

Isaiah 48:

12 Hearken unto me, O Jacob and Israel, my called; I am he; I am the first, I also am the last.

13 Mine hand also hath laid the foundation of the earth, and my right hand hath spanned the heavens: when I call unto them, they stand up together.

14 All ye, assemble yourselves, and hear; which among them hath declared these things? The Lord hath loved him: he will do his pleasure on Babylon, and his arm shall be on the Chaldeans.

15 I, even I, have spoken; yea, I have called him: I have brought him, and he shall make his way prosperous.

16 Come ye near unto me, hear ye this; I have not spoken in secret from the beginning; from the time that it was, there am I: and now the Lord God, and his Spirit, hath sent me.

God is speaking, defining Himself as being the "Alpha and Omega" (same description as Jesus in Revelation 1 and 21) and then in verse 16 He says that "from the time that it was, there am I" and that "the Lord God and the Spirit has sent Me."

God is the Trinity

One God - three persons, united, working as one. (Note that "the Trinity" is another singular plurality.)

When the Trinity is spoken of in Protestant and Catholic religions, it is referring to the relationship of three entities - the Father, the Son and the Holy Spirit.

United together, the three are "God" - truly OUR TRIUNE GOD!

View of some Jews

Many Jews acknowledge the plurality of God, but do not accept the New Testament and the truth that Jesus is the Emmanuel (God with us) and is the "Christ", revealed throughout the Old Testament, that they are still looking forward to coming back and establishing an earthly kingdom.

They are well aware of the plurality of the verbiage used in the Bible for God, but over the years have fallen prey to Satan's deception. Even today, some explain this plurality as being what is called "the Royal We" - as in the language used largely by nobility starting in the 1100s. (https://grammarist. com/usage/royal-we/)

The view of these Jews is that God was expressing "royalty" by using plurality verbiage. Personally, I see a problem with this concept:

The plurality verbiage for God was used throughout the Old Testament by multiple writers from multiple countries across multiple centuries. Though the consistency would confirm the Holy Spirit as writing the whole Bible, it would not make sense for Him to utilize verbiage that would not be common until the 1100s at the time the Old Testament books were written.

God's Word was written so that all who read it would come to know God. To me, it seems that it would defeat His purpose to utilize vernacular that did not exist at the time it was written. God revealed the plurality from the beginning, but the Scribes and Pharisees were the only ones who read it and they had no basis to share the concept to common people. They also did not have the New Testament to explain the Father / Son / Holy Spirit relationship that we have.

Some Jews view the plurality as a multi-facetted view. Hebrew has words (like for water, sky, face) which point out that there is variance in what is seen. (a face can look happy, sad, angry, curious, lost, etc). They see God (Elohim) as plurality in all the multitude/dynamics of relationship with us.

In Deuteronomy 6:4, Moses directly said that Yah-weh is God (Elohim) and is One. This phrase is incorporated into the Shema (one of the primary prayers of Judaism).

In defense of the Jewish explanations, at the time the books were written, in the diverse places and by the myriad of writers all using a plural word to identify a singular God (and singular Lord), this "had" to be a constant "mystery of God" they had to deal with. Our full knowledge of the Trinity (and understanding the plural verbiage) came to us when "the Word became flesh" in the New Testament. Most Jews of today do not acknowledge the New Testament, so they are still locked into the mystery.

The Trinity at work:

(Full view of this is expanded in the chapter "Three Persons?")

Let's look at some attributes of God:

Creates	Controls	Omniscient (all knowing)	Convicts
Plans	Guides	Omnipresent (all present)	Defends
Comforts	Empowers	Omnipotent (all powerful)	

Upon examination of their workings in the Bible, we see that most attributes of "God" can be mostly identified with one of the Trinity individually.

Father	*Son*	*Holy Spirit*
Plans	Creates	Comforts
Is Omniscient	Defends	Empowers
	Controls	Convicts
	Is Omnipotent	Guides
		Is Omnipresent

All three Persons have specific/separate functions and not one individual is the totality of "God"; however, God is credited for the work of each individual.

For example: Genesis says, "God created the Heavens and the Earth". John 1 and Hebrews 1 both specifically say that "all things" were created by the Son.

John 1:

> 3 Through him all things were made; without him nothing was made that has been made.

The Son created all things and it is rightly stated that "God" created them.

Another example: In Acts (5:1-4), Ananias and Sapphira, lied to the Holy Spirit and in so doing "lied to God".

One of Jesus's last commands was for His disciples (then and now) to baptize new believers in the name of the Father, the Son and the Holy Spirit.

Matthew 28:

> 19 Go ye therefore, and teach all nations, baptizing them in the name of the Father, and of the Son, and of the Holy Ghost:
>
> 20 Teaching them to observe all things whatsoever I have commanded you: and, lo, I am with you always, even unto the end of the world. Amen.

It is fascinating to me that Jesus took the time and specifically commanded us to baptize in the name of the Father, the Son and the Holy Ghost. If all three are the same entity, why was it important to Him that we acknowledge all three individually during baptism?

The importance of "how" we view God:

The more we know and understand about anything, be it a person, a job, a project, etc, the better we can interact.

Satan affects all areas of our lives by disrupting our views/perspectives of the things around us – divisions in a family, prejudices at a job, assignments on a project, etc. Satan's job is to destroy our joy any way he can.

Our relation to God is Satan's primary focus. From Adam and Eve in the garden unto today, his purpose has not changed. The less we know and understand about God, the less "power of God" we can use against him. Even as you read this book, Satan will use every idea and concept you have ever heard or believed to deter your researching the possibilities of the views presented herein.

Whether you end up agreeing with what I present is less important than researching for yourself, confirming or amending your beliefs and thereby strengthening your knowledge and your faith.

Expanding your understanding of our Triune God lets you see God in awesome completeness. For many who have viewed only the Father as God and the Son and Spirit as somehow lower than God, hopefully they will come to view God in a new magnificence.

For me, any time I hear or see the word "God", I automatically look to see if I can determine which (or all) of the three is being mentioned. It is my hope that all who read this book will see God in a new light.

We must always use the Holy Spirit's guidance any time we hear the word "God" used to keep in focus which person(s) of the Trinity is actually being referred to; thereby "rightly dividing the Word of Truth" (2 Tim. 2:15).

SUMMARY: THE TRIUNE NATURE OF GOD

The Bible was written with full revelation of the plural nature of God. The Hebrew word "Elohim" (used 2602 times in the OT) is the plural of "El" or "Eloah". As our word "men" is plural of man and the single word "family" denotes a unit of several individuals, "Elohim" denotes multiplicity. The use of the word "Elohim" when "El" and "Eloah" could have been used, indicates that the Bible was given to us for full awareness of the plurality of God - just the spiritual leaders of the past didn't have the Father/Son/Spirit concept which came available with the New Testament and spiritual leaders of today are rarely exposed to the verbiage so clearly presented in the Old Testament.

The confusion about "God".

Satan has inserted his confusion through man's use of language. From the beginning, Satan has twisted words to change man's understanding. In the Garden of Eden he successfully confused Eve with the meaning of "die" (Gen. 3), and he has been confusing man ever since. The more he can water down our understanding of God, the less we are able to stand up against him.

Throughout time, preachers, teachers, Bible translators, etc. have used the word "God" when they refer to works of the Father.

Terms like "God and His Son" are common. This has led many people to think subconsciously that only the Father is God. Anytime they hear the word "God" they automatically visualize the Father and logically subordinate the Son and Holy Spirit. That is how Satan wants it - it makes it hard for us to understand our position "in" Christ when we see Him subordinate to God and not an equal part of God.

Ephesians 2:
10 For we are his workmanship, created in Christ Jesus for good works, which God prepared beforehand, that we should walk in them.

Romans 8:
1 There is therefore now no condemnation to them which are in Christ Jesus, who walk not after the flesh, but after the Spirit. 2 For the law of the Spirit of life in Christ Jesus hath made me free from the law of sin and death.

THREE PERSONS?

We MUST keep in mind that the Father/ Son/Spirit conceptual relationship was created and established as God's way of helping us to relate to the workings of three entities we cannot even fathom in human terms.

In church we stand and sing "God in three persons, blessed Trinity" but, because of limited definition of the Trinity taught in the churches, the "in three persons" part just seems to go away.

Over the years, I began to see the Bible in fascinating perspective. I started seeing separation of the "works" of God – that each member of the Trinity has specific functions which "God" is designated as doing. I can also see where the confusion could be from man's use of words.

   * First, we are dealing with the limited understanding of the "Trinity".

   * Couple that with the concept of God becoming "flesh and dwelling among us". (John 1 says that the Son became flesh and dwelt among us.)

   * Jesus told the disciples to pray "Our Father, which is in heaven". If God was a single entity, then who/what was Jesus praying to throughout His life on earth? God being the Trinity explains it.

   * Both preachers and some writers of books of the Bible use phrases like "God and His Son" which Satan is able to implant logically in people's heads that the Son is subordinate to God and not a part of God. However, as is explained herein, the word "God" refers to any one of them individually AND to all of them collectively.

   * The Son and the Spirit ARE clearly subordinate to the Father, but are still an equal part of "God".

Why do we claim three persons to be God?

Throughout the Bible, each member of the Trinity is acknowledged as God. (Technically, they are all "part" of God - three united entities, working as one!)

The Father is readily acknowledged as God. I have heard of no one denying the Father as God, so I will concur with that fact. The main point to pick up is that the Father is clearly in charge.

The Son was obedient unto death

Philippians 2:
8 Jesus, creator of all things, was "obedient to the point of death, even the death of the cross"

The Holy Spirit works as directed.

John 16:
13 When the Spirit of truth comes, he will guide you into all the truth, for he will not speak on his own authority, but whatever he hears he will speak, and he will declare to you the things that are to come.

GOD THE FATHER:
Is Omniscient: All knowing. Only the Father knows "everything".

Matthew 24:
36 But concerning that day and hour no one knows, not even the angels of heaven, nor the Son, but the Father only.

Is "In charge": Jesus also said that He can do nothing that the Father does not authorize.

John 14:
10 The words that I say to you I do not speak on my own authority, but the Father who dwells in me does his works.

Plans: Just as the Father planned Jesus's time on Earth, He has a purpose for every one of us.

Ephesians 2:
10 For we are his workmanship, created in Christ Jesus for good works, which God prepared beforehand, that we should walk in them.

Objective: That all who choose to love the Son can come into His presence when we die.

2 Corinthians 5:
8 We are confident, I say, and willing rather to be absent from the body and to be present with the Lord.

When we get saved, He does not call us home. We are still here to fulfill His pre-planned purpose for us, so that all should come to know Christ and ultimately go into the presence of the Father with Him.

GOD THE SON:

Is "The Word": Throughout time, God spoke to man through the head of the family, judges, prophets, etc.; but ultimately through the Son (termed "the Word" because His coming to Earth established the final word on how man is to relate to God).

John 1:
1 In the beginning was the Word; and the Word was with God, and the Word was God.

14 … the Word became flesh and dwelt among us.

Is God: "The Word" was with God, was God, created all things, became flesh and dwelt among us.

Is Omnipotent: All powerful. All things were created by Him according to the directions of the Father. By the word of His power He controls the elements.

Hebrews 1:
3 Who being the brightness of his glory, and the express image of his person, and upholding all things by the word of his power, when he had by himself purged our sins, sat down on the right hand of the Majesty on high:

Genesis says "God created the earth". John 1 and Colossians 1 clearly state that the Son created the earth. If "the Son" is not equally part of "God", then Genesis is a lie.

Genesis 1:
1 In the beginning God created the heavens and the earth

Colossians 1: (Paul speaking on the supremacy of Christ)
16 For by Him all things were created: things in heaven and on earth, visible and invisible, whether thrones or powers or rulers or authorities; all things were created by Him and for Him.

17 He is before all things, and in Him all things hold together.

Philippians 2:6, Colossians 2:9, and Hebrews 1:8, all establish the Son as God:

Philipians 2:
5 Let this mind be in you which was also in Christ Jesus,

6 who, being in the form of God, did not consider it robbery to be equal with God,

Colosians 2:
9 For in Him (Christ) dwells all the fullness of the Godhead bodily;

Hebrews. 1: (The Father speaking of the Son)
8 But about the Son He says, "Your throne, O God, will last for ever and ever, and righteousness will be the scepter of your kingdom."

John 1:
18 No one has ever seen God, but the one and only Son, who is himself God and is in closest relationship with the Father, has made him known.

Logic also supports that the Son is God. Genesis 3 says that Adam and Eve walked with God. In John 6:46, Jesus said that no man has seen the Father.

John 6:
46 No one has seen the Father except the one who is from God; only he has seen the Father.

Since Jesus cannot lie and be without sin, Adam and Eve had to have walked with the Son and thereby confirming Jesus as God.

Jesus declared Himself as "The Almighty God" in Genesis 35 when He re-appeared to Jacob and changed his name to Israel.

Genesis 35:
9 And God appeared unto Jacob again, when he came out of Padanaram, and blessed him.

10 And God said unto him, Thy name is Jacob: thy name shall not be called any more Jacob, but Israel shall be thy name: and he called his name Israel.

11 And God said unto him, I am God Almighty: be fruitful and multiply; a nation and a company of nations shall be of thee, and kings shall come out of thy loins

12 And the land which I gave Abraham and Isaac, to thee I will give it, and to thy seed after thee will I give the land.

13 And God went up from him in the place where he talked with him.

Jacob first wrestled with "God" (Gen 32:22-32), then "God" reappeared to him and changed his name (Gen 35:9-13).

Again, since "no man has seen the Father", Jacob must have been with The Son who declared Himself to be God Almighty (omnipotent).

In John 20:28-29, Thomas called Jesus "God".

John 20:

28 And Thomas answered and said unto him, My Lord and my God.

29 Jesus saith unto him, Thomas, because thou hast seen me, thou hast believed: blessed are they that have not seen, and yet have believed.

Jesus did not correct Thomas when he called Jesus "God", thus Jesus acknowledged it as a correct statement. If Jesus is not an equal part of God, then His accepting false credit as God makes Him fallible and thereby unable to be Savior.

In Isaiah 48:12-16, "God", who created all things and is the "I AM", was sent by the Lord God and the Holy Spirit.

Are the Father and the Son the same person?

Jesus clearly states that He and the Father are united as one, but also points out that they are individual and separate.

Jesus is "the way" to the Father

John 14:

5 Thomas said to him, "Lord, we don't know where you are going, so how can we know the way?"

6 Jesus answered, "I am the way and the truth and the life. No one comes to the Father except through me.

7 If you really know me, you will know my Father as well. From now on, you do know him and have seen him."

8 Philip said, "Lord, show us the Father and that will be enough for us."

9 Jesus answered: "Don't you know me, Philip, even after I have been among you such a long time? Anyone who has seen me has seen the Father. How can you say, 'Show us the Father'?

10 Don't you believe that I am in the Father, and that the Father is in me? The words I say to you I do not speak on my own authority. Rather, it is the Father, living in me, who is doing his work.

11 Believe me when I say that I am in the Father and the Father is in me; or at least believe on the evidence of the works themselves.

12 Very truly I tell you, whoever believes in me will do the works I have been doing, and they will do even greater things than these, because I am going to the Father.

13 And I will do whatever you ask in my name, so that the Father may be glorified in the Son.

Jesus never said "I am the Father" (Satan likes for us to stop at v.9, but Jesus continued.) He was clear that He is "in" the Father and that the Father is "in" Him; that He can only do what the Father "living in Him" authorizes; that He is not the Father, but He is going "TO" the Father and He is "the only way" to the Father.

If Jesus was physically the Father, then all Jesus said from v. 10 to the end of the chapter is wasted breath because He consistently refers to the Father as a separate person than Himself.

Jesus was so unified with the Father that He was a virtual reflection of the Father. Jesus pointed out to His disciples that they should see and know the Father by what they see in Him.

John 14:

18 I will not leave you as orphans; I will come to you.

19 Before long, the world will not see me anymore, but you will see me. Because I live, you also will live.

20 On that day you will realize that I am in my Father, and you are in me, and I am in you.

21 Whoever has my commands and keeps them is the one who loves me. The one who loves me will be loved by my Father, and I too will love them and show myself to them."

22 Then Judas (not Judas Iscariot) said, "But, Lord, why do you intend to show yourself to us and not to the world?"

23 Jesus replied, "Anyone who loves me will obey my teaching. My Father will love them, and we will come to them and make our home with them.

24 Anyone who does not love me will not obey my teaching. These words you hear are not my own; they belong to the Father who sent me.

Jesus again pointed out the relationship of being "in" the Father as He told the disciples that they will be "in" Him just as He is "in" the Father, and vise-versa. He also pointed out that the Father sent Him. (If He "IS" the Father, then He sent Himself?????)

As Jesus explained to the disciples, we should live our lives in such a way that others should see and come to know Jesus through seeing us, Jesus should be in us just as the Father was in Him.

John 14:

27 Peace I leave with you; my peace I give you. I do not give to you as the world gives. Do not let your hearts be troubled and do not be afraid.

28 "You heard me say, 'I am going away and I am coming back to you.' If you loved me, you would be glad that I am going to the Father, for the Father is greater than I.

29 I have told you now before it happens, so that when it does happen you will believe.

30 I will not say much more to you, for the prince of this world is coming. He has no hold over me,

31 but he comes so that the world may learn that I love the Father and do exactly what my Father has commanded me. Come now; let us leave.

If the Father and the Son are the same person, why did Jesus go to such length to point out to His disciples that He is the way "to" the Father and that He does NOT speak on His own authority (v. 10), but only does what the Father commands Him to do? Being the same person also conflicts with v. 28 where Jesus says He is "going to" the Father and that the Father is greater than He.

It is easy for Satan to attack the idea of the Son being God and to deceive us into thinking that He is not. Satan's objective is for us to see Jesus as separate from God so that we never realize our position "in Christ" (v. 20 and Rom 8:1-2) to its full perspective. Just as the Father was in Him, He said that He would be in us.

The Father is superior to the Son.

Every singular plurality has authority structure. A "team" has a captain, an "army has a general, a company has a president, etc. The Father is the authority for "God".

Jesus said multiple times that He only did what the Father said and directed. (John 5:16-47)

Jesus, creator of all things, was "obedient to the point of death, even the death of the cross" (Phil. 2:8)

Jesus was obedient to the authority of the Father.

GOD THE HOLY SPIRIT:

Like the Son, Satan loves for us to misunderstand the Holy Spirit.

In our human mind, Satan is persistent to try to keep us "in the dark" about the full function of the Holy Spirit. Without the Holy Spirit, we cannot even get saved. It is VERY IMPORTANT for us to truly get to know Him personally.

The Holy Spirit:
* Omnipresent: All present at all times
* Was sent by the Father and the Son
* Dwells in all who accept Christ as Savior
* Is the Advocate for the cause of Christ
* Exalts the Son for the glory of the Father
* Is the seal given to us by the Father until the "day of redemption"

Is the Holy Spirit a person or an "it"?

Satan would love for us to see the Holy Spirit as some kind of "sci-fi" life force. Our seeing Him as a force and not a person, diminishes our ability to have a true personal relationship with Him.

Jesus was clear in His relation and view of the Holy Spirit. In "every" reference Jesus makes, He uses personal pronouns. Jesus never refers to the Holy Spirit as an "it".

John 16:

7 But very truly I tell you, it is for your good that I am going away. Unless I go away, the Advocate will not come to you; but if I go, I will send him to you.

8 When he comes, he will prove the world to be in the wrong about sin and righteousness and judgment:

9 about sin, because people do not believe in me;

10 about righteousness, because I am going to the Father, where you can see me no longer;

11 and about judgment, because the prince of this world now stands condemned.

12 "I have much more to say to you, more than you can now bear.

13 But when he, the Spirit of truth, comes, he will guide you into all the truth. He will not speak on his own; he will speak only what he hears, and he will tell you what is yet to come.

14 He will glorify me because it is from me that he will receive what he will make known to you.

15 All that belongs to the Father is mine. That is why I said the Spirit will receive from me what he will make known to you."

As a "person", the Holy Spirit can be grieved (Eph. 4:30), lied to (Acts 5:3-4) and quenched (1 Thess 5:19)

Ephesians 4:

30 And grieve not the holy Spirit of God, whereby ye are sealed unto the day of redemption.

Acts 5:

3 But Peter said, "Ananias, why has Satan filled your heart to lie to the Holy Spirit … "

1 Thessalonians 5:

19 Quench not the Spirit.

As a person, we have a far stronger relationship (a personal relationship) with the Holy Spirit and it increases the work He can do through us. Your relationship with the Holy Spirit IS most important, so strive to get to know Him "personally"!

Satan definitely wants to hinder our relationship with the Holy Spirit because the Holy Spirit empowers us against him. Our seeing the Holy Spirit as an "it" does not let us reach our full potential as a weapon against Satan.

Is the Holy Spirit God?

The Holy Spirit is specifically called "God" in Acts 5:3-4; 1 Corinthians 3:16; 2 Corinthians 3:17-18; Genesis 1:2c, 26a and Job 33:4. Acts 28:25-27 and Hebrews 3:7-9 also show the Holy Spirit to be God.

Acts 5:

3 Then Peter said, "Ananias, how is it that Satan has so filled your heart that you have lied to the Holy Spirit and have kept for yourself some of the money you received for the land?

4 Didn't it belong to you before it was sold? And after it was sold, wasn't the money at your disposal? What made you think of doing such a thing? You have not lied to men but to God."

1 John 4:15: God dwells within all who confess the Son.

1 Corinthians 3:16: the Holy Spirit dwells in us.

The "Word of God" (the Bible) was given through men by the Holy Spirit

2 Timothy 3:

16 All scripture is given by inspiration of God, and is profitable for doctrine, for reproof, for correction, for instruction in righteousness:

2 Peter 1:

16 Knowing this first, that no prophecy of the scripture is of any private interpretation.

17 For the prophecy came not in old time by the will of man: but holy men of God spake as they were moved by the Holy Ghost.

Would the Bible, given to men by the Holy Spirit, be "The Word of God" if the the Holy Spirit is NOT God?

The Holy Spirit is omnipresent – in all places at the same time.

Psalms 139:

7 Whither shall I go from thy spirit? or whither shall I flee from thy presence?

8 If I ascend up into heaven, thou art there: if I make my
bed in hell, behold, thou art there.

Jesus said "Our Father which art in heaven" and "I go to be with the
Father." Several scriptures state that the Son is sitting at the right hand of
the Father acting as our advocate. The Bible shows us that the Father is on
the heavenly throne with the Son at His side.

Hebrews 10:
12 But when this priest had offered for all time one sacrifice
for sins, he sat down at the right hand of God,

Romans 8:
34 Who is he that condemns? It is Christ that died, yea
rather, that is risen again, who is even at the right hand of
God, who also makes intercession for us.

Jesus said that He went to prepare us a place so that where He "IS",
"THERE" we will be also. This seems to show that the Father and Son are
not omnipresent in the physical sense that the Holy Spirit is.

My parents (both deceased) live in me and are with me "in spirit". Because
of my knowledge and relationships with them, they will always be with
me. However, this is an emotional and mental state of being – they are not
physically with me.

Likewise, Jesus and the Father (because of my relationship and knowledge
of them) are with me "in spirit". Unfortunately (... or fortunately) I don't
get to have conversations with my parents like I do with God. The amazing
thing about the Holy Spirit is that He is with me physically, just as Jesus
said the Spirit would be.

Our understanding of the ability of the Holy Spirit to be in all places at the
same time, increases OUR ability to be used by God. The Holy Spirit was
given to us, not only as a seal to our promise of eternal life, but also as our
guide and protector during our life here on Earth. The reason we are still
here, and not taken to Heaven the moment we accept Christ, is for us to
be a living testimony pointing others to God. Satan has free reign in this
world and we must have the power of the Holy Spirit to keep Satan at bay.

When Jesus was in His earthly form, the Bible says that He was filled with
the Holy Spirit. The Holy Spirit LED Jesus into the desert after His baptism
to be tested. The Bible speaks several times of Jesus being led by the Holy
Spirit.

Luke 4:

14 And Jesus returned in the power of the Spirit into Galilee: and there went out a fame of him through all the region round about.

15 And he taught in their synagogues, being glorified of all.

16 And he came to Nazareth, where he had been brought up: and, as his custom was, he went into the synagogue on the sabbath day, and stood up for to read.

17 And there was delivered unto him the book of the prophet Esaias. And when he had opened the book, he found the place where it was written,

18 The Spirit of the Lord is upon me, because he hath anointed me to preach the gospel to the poor; he hath sent me to heal the brokenhearted, to preach deliverance to the captives, and recovering of sight to the blind, to set at liberty them that are bruised,

19 To preach the acceptable year of the Lord.

20 And he closed the book, and he gave it again to the minister, and sat down. And the eyes of all them that were in the synagogue were fastened on him.

21 And he began to say unto them, This day is this scripture fulfilled in your ears.

Jesus acknowledged that He was the one "anointed and empowered by the Holy Spirit" that fulfilled that prophesy.

Through the Holy Spirit, Jesus was able to know what those around Him were thinking.

John 1:

46 And Nathanael said to him, "Can anything good come out of Nazareth?" Philip said to him, "Come and see."

47 Jesus saw Nathanael coming toward Him, and said of him, "Behold, an Israelite indeed, in whom is no deceit!"

48 Nathanael said to Him, "How do You know me?" Jesus answered and said to him, "Before Philip called you, when you were under the fig tree, I saw you."

49 Nathanael answered and said to Him, "Rabbi, You are the Son of God! You are the King of Israel!"

50 Jesus answered and said to him, "Because I said to you, 'I saw you under the fig tree,' do you believe? You will see greater things than these."

Jesus was able to "know" what was in the minds of the Pharisees, the disciples, etc. because the Holy Spirit told Him. He saw Nathanael, not because He was there, but because the Holy Spirit was there and showed Him.

Likewise, we receive our words of knowledge, prophecy, discernment, etc. because the Holy Spirit gives it to us. How does a person with the gift of giving "just happen to know" exactly how much to give someone? It is because the Holy Spirit is with the other person at the same time. We receive specific words of exhortation because the Holy Spirit is with the recipient simultaneous with us.

When we let the Holy Spirit have control, He utilizes His omnipresence to exalt the Son to the glory of the Father through us.

How do we receive the Holy Spirit?

Ephesians 1:

12 That we should be to the praise of his glory, who first trusted in Christ.

13 In whom ye also trusted, after that ye heard the word of truth, the gospel of your salvation: in whom also after that ye believed, ye were sealed with that holy Spirit of promise,

14 Which is the earnest of our inheritance until the redemption of the purchased possession, unto the praise of his glory.

The moment we truly "believe and accept" the gospel of truth (that Christ paid the penalty of our sins with His blood) the Holy Spirit is given to us as a seal (finalized unbreakable agreement) unto the day of redemption (when we ultimately arrive in the presence of the Father and Son).

PRAYER (Here is where it gets good!)

If the Father is in heaven and the Son is at the right hand of the Father, how does the Father and Son hear our prayers? Because the Holy Spirit is right there with them at the same time He is with us. The Bible says that God knows our prayers even before we put them into words. How? Because the Holy Spirit is with us. Being an equal part of God and being in the simultaneous presence of the Father and Son makes prayer happen.

Galatians 5:

16 But I say, walk by the Spirit, and you will not gratify the desires of the flesh.

17 For the desires of the flesh are against the Spirit, and

the desires of the Spirit are against the flesh, for these are opposed to each other, to keep you from doing the things you want to do.

18 But if you are led by the Spirit, you are not under the law.

When we sin against the Holy Spirit, we let our worldly self-rule. The Holy Spirit steps back and sorta says "OK, do it your way." We technically, turn off the Holy Spirit working in us – we have "quenched the Holy Spirit" and, since the Holy Spirit is omnipresent, we cut off our communication with God. We stifle our prayers with the Father and Son and hinder their blessings and the workings of their spiritual gifts through us.

One of the keys to understanding the work of the Holy Spirit is the warning the Bible gives us "to quench not the Holy Spirit!" (1 Thess. 5:19)

Our having a personal relationship with the Holy Spirit amplifies His ability to work through us. Unrepentant sin quenches the Spirit and blocks Him from working.

Indwelling of the Spirit / Being filled with the Spirit

Just because the Holy Spirit is sent to dwell in us until we are redeemed by the Father, that does not mean that we are "filled" with the Spirit.

A very simplistic explanation:

The Holy Spirit dwells in every person that has acknowledged the Son as their Savior. He is constantly working to develop us into a living reflection of Christ.

When we are filled with the Spirit, we allow Him to take total control. We follow His directions without challenge and we are empowered with spiritual gifts that allow us to go on the offense against the works of Satan.

"Indwelling" allows us to excel in the earthly realm and "filling" allows us to excel in the spiritual realm.

HOW DOES GOD'S BEING A TRI-UNITY AFFECT US?

Since Man was made in the image of God, we are also a tri-unity.

Man has three parts – mind, body and spirit. Each part has specific and separate functions and we are not a complete person without each one. Our mind determines and controls (rules) our actions, our body executes them and our spirit (our conscience and will) decides right and wrong based on the rules established by our mind. If any of the three is not functioning, then the person is not complete.

Any person that does not have God in their life is ruled by natural instinct and insight. Satan has full control over this "natural man." (1 Cor. 2:14) They live totally under the humanistic law of "What's in it for me?" and "If it feels good do it." Their life is total sin and the wages of sin, for this person, is eternal death. (ie. the complete separation from the Father for eternity.)

When we accept Jesus Christ as our Savior and make Him Lord of our lives, then the Holy Spirit moves into us as a seal (promise) of our salvation from eternal death. (Eph. 1:13,14; 4:30) As a "spiritual man", in the image of God, we take on the mind of the all-knowing Father, we become a part of the body of the Son and we live in harmony with the Holy Spirit.

When we depend on the Holy Spirit to do His job and direct our lives, He makes His decisions for us based on the Father's rules. This is the condition that God wants for us. It is called "spiritual man."

Romans 8:

1 There is therefore now no condemnation to them which are in Christ Jesus, who walk not after the flesh, but after the Spirit.

2 For the law of the Spirit of life in Christ Jesus hath made me free from the law of sin and death.

3 For what the law could not do, in that it was weak through the flesh, God sending his own Son in the likeness of sinful flesh, and for sin, condemned sin in the flesh:

4 That the righteousness of the law might be fulfilled in us, who walk not after the flesh, but after the Spirit.

5 For they that are after the flesh do mind the things of the flesh; but they that are after the Spirit the things of the Spirit.

6 For to be carnally minded is death; but to be spiritually minded is life and peace.

7 Because the carnal mind is enmity against God: for it is not subject to the law of God, neither indeed can be.

8 So then they that are in the flesh cannot please God.

9 But ye are not in the flesh, but in the Spirit, if so be that the Spirit of God dwell in you. Now if any man have not the Spirit of Christ, he is none of his.

10 And if Christ be in you, the body is dead because of sin; but the Spirit is life because of righteousness.

11 But if the Spirit of him that raised up Jesus from the dead

dwell in you, he that raised up Christ from the dead shall also quicken your mortal bodies by his Spirit that dwelleth in you.

12 Therefore, brethren, we are debtors, not to the flesh, to live after the flesh.

13 For if ye live after the flesh, ye shall die: but if ye through the Spirit do mortify the deeds of the body, ye shall live.

14 For as many as are led by the Spirit of God, they are the sons of God.

15 For ye have not received the spirit of bondage again to fear; but ye have received the Spirit of adoption, whereby we cry, Abba, Father.

16 The Spirit himself beareth witness with our spirit, that we are the children of God:

The Holy Spirit "bears witness WITH our spirit" of our being a child of God and is to teach us, guide us, empower us for battle with Satan, etc. One of His main jobs is to help us through communication to the Father. Living a spiritual (Spirit filled) life allows the Father to provide us with blessings beyond our natural understanding.

Romans 8:

26 Likewise the Spirit also helps our infirmities: for we know not what we should pray for as we ought: but the Spirit makes intercession for us with groanings which cannot be uttered.

27 And he that searches the hearts knows what is the mind of the Spirit, because he makes intercession for the saints according to the will of God.

God hears our prayers "through" the Holy Spirit. When we quench the Spirit, we cut off our prayers to God.

Isaiah 59:

1 Behold, the Lord's hand is not shortened, that it cannot save; neither his ear heavy, that it cannot hear:

2 But your iniquities have separated between you and your God, and your sins have hid his face from you, that he will not hear.

When we, who have accepted Jesus as our Savior, have unrepentant sin in our lives; we let our spirit over-rule the Holy Spirit. We become a "Carnal Man". Even after we have been indwelled with the Holy Spirit, we can quench the Spirit and live as natural man.

1 Corinthians 3:

1 And I, brethren, could not speak unto you as unto spiritual, but as unto carnal, even as unto babes in Christ.

2 I have fed you with milk, and not with meat: for hitherto ye were not able to bear it, neither yet now are ye able.

3 For ye are yet carnal: for whereas there is among you envying, and strife, and divisions, are ye not carnal, and walk as men?

In this condition, we break our communications to the Father because we have shut out the Person whose job it is to intercede for us.

Romans 8:

5 Those who live according to the flesh have their minds set on what the flesh desires; but those who live in accordance with the Spirit have their minds set on what the Spirit desires.

6 The mind governed by the flesh is death, but the mind governed by the Spirit is life and peace.

7 The mind governed by the flesh is hostile to God; it does not submit to God's law, nor can it do so.

8 Those who are in the realm of the flesh cannot please God.

While we are in this "carnal" state, we forfeit all the blessings that the Father would have presented us during that time. Thus the "wages of sin" for a Carnal Man is the "death" of blessings and spiritual power, plus you earn the consequences of those sins. You lose un-told blessings and you still must face the physical "reaping" of your sins.

For example: You can be spiritually forgiven for committing adultery by asking in a spirit of remorse and repentance; however, you will not be released from consequences like aids or pregnancy.

Though King David was forgiven by God for his sins with Bathsheba and Uriah, he still reaped the consequences of the loss of his son Absalom.

Galations 5:

16 This I say then, Walk in the Spirit, and ye shall not fulfill the lust of the flesh.

17 For the flesh lusteth against the Spirit, and the Spirit against the flesh: and these are contrary the one to the other: so that ye cannot do the things that ye would.

18 But if ye be led of the Spirit, ye are not under the law.

SUMMARY: THREE PERSONS
Key Attributes: Omniscient, Omipotent, Omnipresent

The Father is omniscient. Only the Father knows everything.

Mark 13:
32 "But concerning that day or that hour, no one knows, not even the angels in heaven, nor the Son, but only the Father.

The Son is omnipotent. He created everything that exists.

Colossians 1:
6 For by him were all things created, that are in heaven, and that are in earth, visible and invisible, whether they be thrones, or dominions, or principalities, or powers: all things were created by him, and for him:

The Holy Spirit is omnipresent. He is in all places at the same time. (The Father is in heaven and the Son is at the right hand of the Father.)

Psalms 139:
7 Whither shall I go from thy spirit? or whither shall I flee from thy presence?

8 If I ascend up into heaven, thou art there: if I make my bed in hell, behold, thou art there.

The Father, who is omniscient (knows all things), has a plan and destiny for each of us. As any loving father, He wants the best for us; but as a parent, He also yields blessing in response to obedience and discipline for disobedience. (A child who disobeys all week cannot expect the car keys to go out with friends on the weekend. Right?)

The Son, who is omnipotent (all powerful), created all things (including us) and came in the flesh to personally provide the way to the Father. As creator, we give Him love; as Savior, we give Him gratitude; and as Lord, we give Him honor and allegiance. Jesus gave us this life and made the way for eternal life, but it is making Him Lord that gives us the best of this life now.

The Holy Spirit, who is omnipresent (in all places at all times), was sent to empower us against Satan and give us the tools and guidance for us to exalt the Son to the glory of the Father. The Holy Spirit moves at the instruction of the Father and Son. You should strive to be "in tune" with Him 24/7. Because of human nature, it is hard; but being aware of His constant indwelling presence, and seeking His daily empowerment, will give you an edge in having a walk that serves and honors God.

THREE SINS?

Sin is often defined as "anything that comes between you and God". Seeing God as our Triune God helps you focus on the affect and severity of sin in your life.

One Sunday while teaching a single adult class, I read the verse (Hebrews 4:5) "Jesus was tempted in ALL WAYS as are we, yet without sin." A guy sitting near the back of the room stood up, slammed his Bible into the floor and headed for the door.

I said "Whoa! Hey guy, – what's the matter?"

He firmly stated back, "Jesus was never married! He could NOT have been tempted to cheat on his wife! The Bible is a lie! I am out of here!"

I acknowledged that what he was saying sounds VERY logical, but I stood firm on Titus 1:2, that God cannot lie. I told him I did not have the answer, but I told him I would research it and got him to agree to give me a week to work on it and to come back the next Sunday. (As I recall, that next Sunday was one of the larger attendance days as it seemed everyone was interested in what I would find out.)

Needless to say, my prayer time and Bible study went into overdrive.

I began with the statement: "Jesus was tempted in all ways as are we..." I looked for all places where Jesus was tempted and found Matthew 4 and Luke 4 – where Jesus was led into the desert to be tempted by Satan.

The Bible emphasizes three temptations: He was tempted to make bread out of a rock, to bow down to Satan to receive kingdoms and to throw Himself off of the top of the temple in Jerusalem.

I saw no correlation with cheating on a wife. Then, what seemed to come out of nowhere, the Holy Spirit revealed 1 John 2:16 to me.

1 John 2:

16 This is that which is in the world: the lust of the eyes, the lust of the flesh and the pride of life.

I still did not see the whole picture until Galatians 5:19 – 21 was revealed to me.

Galatians 5:

19 Now the works of the flesh are manifest, which are these; adultery, fornication, uncleanness, lasciviousness,

20 Idolatry, witchcraft, hatred, variance, emulations, wrath, strife, seditions, heresies,

21 Envyings, murders, drunkenness, revelings, and such ...

The "works of the flesh" manifest themselves as what we typically call sins. Likewise, "lust of the eyes" and "pride of life" manifest the same way. It does not matter what our manifestation is, the spiritual "sin" takes place in our heart long before the worldly manifestation.

Matt 15:

19 For out of the heart come evil thoughts, murder, adultery, sexual immorality, theft, false witness, slander.

God judges the heart:

1 Kings 8:

39 Then hear in heaven your dwelling place and forgive and act and render to each whose heart you know, according to all his ways (for you, you only, know the hearts of all the children of mankind)

Jeremiah 17:

9 The heart is deceitful above all things, and desperately sick; who can understand it?

10 I the Lord search the heart and test the mind, to give every man according to his ways, according to the fruit of his deeds.

Psalms 19:

14 Let the words of my mouth and the meditation of my heart be acceptable in your sight, O Lord, my rock and my redeemer.

Psalms 44:

21 Would not God discover this? For he knows the secrets of the heart.

Psalms 51:

10 Create in me a clean heart, O God, and renew a right spirit within me.

Proverbs 4:

23 Keep your heart with all vigilance, for from it flow the springs of life.

Hebrews 4:

12 For the word of God is living and active, sharper than any two-edged sword, piercing to the division of soul and of spirit, of joints and of marrow, and discerning the thoughts and intentions of the heart.

Jesus said that to "look" upon a woman with lust in your heart, is equal in God's eyes to the physical manifestation.

Matthew 5:

28 But I tell you that anyone who looks at a woman lustfully has already committed adultery with her in his heart.

Sin against God occurs in our heart. The sin then manifests itself into the actions that we call sin. This explains why a "little" lie is EQUAL to murder from God's view - the sin has already been committed "in our hearts" long before the action is taken.

The sins against God are lust of the flesh, lust of the eyes and pride of life. All actions we "call" sin are the manifestations of one of these three sins against God in our heart.

Lust of the flesh > actions to fulfill physical desires

Lust of the eyes > actions to fulfill personal ambitions

Pride of life > actions to satisfy personal feelings

The manifestations of sin are the worldly expression of the sin in our heart. Every "manifestation" of sin is equal as they are all a result of one of the three sins in the heart. In the following examples, the manifestations are the same, but the sin that caused the action for each is different:

MANIFESTATION	SIN
(worldly action)	(heart motivation)

Murder:

David killed Bathsheba's husband	Lust of the flesh
Sons killed fathers for the throne	Lust of the eyes
Cain killed Abel	Pride of life

<u>Lie:</u>

Get favors of the opposite sex	Lust of the flesh
To get a better job	Lust of the eyes
To brag	Pride of life

<u>Cheat on spouse:</u>

Sexual attraction	Lust of the flesh
To get a promotion from a boss	Lust of the eyes
Everyone does it, why shouldn't I?	Pride of life

All worldly actions we call sin are actually manifestations of one of the three sins of the heart.

EVE succumbed to all three sins.

Genesis 3:

6 When the woman saw that the fruit of the tree was good for food (lust of the flesh) and pleasing to the eye (lust of the eyes), and also desirable for gaining wisdom (pride of life), she took some and ate it.

When Jesus was tempted of Satan in the desert, the Bible emphasized three temptations: Turning the rock to bread would have fulfilled "lust of the flesh"; bowing down to Satan to gain kingdoms would have been "lust of the eyes"; and throwing Himself from the temple (where thousands had come to worship God) so that the people could see His angels save Him, He would show off His position and power and would have committed "pride of life".

* Jesus WAS tempted in the same way as are we, yet without sin. *

Sin is anything we do against God, thus we can sin against the Father, the Son or the Holy Spirit.

The Father has a perfect plan for our life. When we take actions to fulfill personal ambitions of our own, we commit "lust of the eyes."

The Son created us, lived sinless in the flesh, and died a physical death so we could use our bodies perfectly. When we take actions to fulfill physical desires, we commit "lust of the flesh."

The Holy Spirit lives in us to show and guide us in the perfect way we are to live. When we do things our own way, we commit "pride of life."

The Three Sins:

Lust of the eyes = sin against the Father;

Lust of the flesh = sin against the Son;

Pride of life = sin against the Holy Spirit;

All three are sin against "God".

Warning: THE WAGES OF SIN IS DEATH! (Romans 6:23)

We readily share this verse with lost people as we point out that if we die without Christ we will be separated from the Father forever. However, this verse was presented to people who had already accepted Christ. Let's look at the verse in context.

Romans 6:

22 But now being made free from sin, and become servants to God, ye have your fruit unto holiness, and the end everlasting life.

23 For the wages of sin is death; but the gift of God is eternal life through Jesus Christ our Lord.

So, Christians can reap the wages of sin? Absolutely! It is possible for us to allow sin to overtake us. When we have a "pet" sin that we allow to continue (especially when God has directly admonished us about it), we put ourself in position to reap the wages of sin.

(How long do you let your child disobey before you administer discipline?)

When we reach a point that our sin quenches the Spirit within us, then we are defined as carnally minded. The Bible is clear that while a person is in a carnal state (living with unrepentant sins), he is dead spiritually.

Romans 8:

6 For to be carnally minded is death; but to be spiritually minded is life and peace.

7 Because the carnal mind is enmity against God: for it is not subject to the law of God, neither indeed can be.

8 So then they that are in the flesh cannot please God.

9 But ye are not in the flesh, but in the Spirit, if so be that the Spirit of God dwell in you. Now if any man have not the Spirit of Christ, he is none of his.

10 And if Christ be in you, the body is dead because of sin; but the Spirit is life because of righteousness.

11 But if the Spirit of him that raised up Jesus from the dead dwell in you, he that raised up Christ from the dead shall also quicken your mortal bodies by his Spirit that dwelleth in you.

12 Therefore, brethren, we are debtors, not to the flesh, to live after the flesh.

13 For if ye live after the flesh, ye shall die: but if ye through the Spirit do mortify the deeds of the body, ye shall live.

In a carnal state, you quench the Spirit and turn off your source of spiritual power and blessings. Be it for a few minutes, a few days, or for however long; you lose all spiritual blessings that God presents to you during that time because you are unable to spiritually see them. Those blessing are dead and gone, but you are also spiritually dead in your ability to do the work the Father has you here to do.

To be spiritually dead (consumed with "pet" sin) does occur while you are physically alive. Don't let Satan twist God's words. (Adam and Eve did not die physically when they ate the fruit, but they did die spiritually.)

Satan lied to Eve in the garden by twisting the meaning of the word "die". The wages of her sins against God was being kicked out of the garden and to live in toil and torment. Don't let Satan do the same to you. Don't think for a minute that you won't reap the wages of your sins.

Galatians 5:
16 This I say then, Walk in the Spirit, and ye shall not fulfill the lust of the flesh.

(… or lust of the eyes, or pride of life.)

The Unpardonable Sin
There is only one sin that cannot be forgiven: to blaspheme the Holy Spirit.

Matthew 12:
31 "Therefore I say to you, every sin and blasphemy will be forgiven men, but the blasphemy against the Spirit will not be forgiven men.

32 Anyone who speaks a word against the Son of Man, it will be forgiven him; but whoever speaks against the Holy Spirit, it will not be forgiven him, either in this age or in the age to come.

Blasphemy is a deliberate act of disrespect and disregard of something or someone. When Jesus was on trial in the Sanhedrin and acknowledged Himself as being the Son of God, He was charged with blasphemy against God.

To blaspheme the Holy Spirit, to totally disregard and disrespect Him, blocks Him from being able to lead that person to the Son. Without the Son, there cannot be forgiveness. Without forgiveness, there is no salvation.

There can be no salvation if you blaspheme the Holy Spirit in your heart.

SUMMARY: THREE SINS:

The Three Sins:
Lust of the eyes = sin against the Father;

Lust of the flesh = sin against the Son;

Pride of life = sin against the Holy Spirit;

All three are sin against "God".

The wages of sin is death! (Romans 6:23)
This death is spiritual - not physical.

For a lost person, it is eternal seperation from the Father.

For a Christian, it is temporary seperation from the power of the Holy Spirit; becoming carnal, thus spiritually dead (Romans 8:6-13)

The Unpardonable Sin
There is only one sin that cannot be forgiven: to blaspheme the Holy Spirit.

THREE SALVATIONS?

God being three persons led me to realize that each of the three have distinct work in our salvation. In the Bible, we see our salvation identified with three terms: "justification", "sanctification" and "glorification".

Free will and salvation

Would you prefer being around people who have to be around you or people that choose to be around you?

God is surrounded by created beings that have to be there. Man was created with free will so that those that choose to be with God are rewarded with eternal life in His presence.

It is sad that more people choose the world over God.

Luke 7:

13 "Enter through the narrow gate. For wide is the gate and broad is the road that leads to destruction, and many enter through it.

14 But small is the gate and narrow the road that leads to life, and only a few find it.

The process established for us to join God in heaven is called salvation and it comes in three parts: justification, glorification and sanctification.

Justification

The ultimate penalty of sin is eternal separation from the Father. Sin cannot stand in the presence of the Father, thus the Son gave himself as the blood sacrifice to justify us and prepared us spiritually to go into the Father's presence.

Through justification we are saved from the penalty of sin. The Son paid for our sin by shedding His blood at His death on the cross. He died ONCE and paid the debt for all people forever.

Romans 5:

1 Therefore, having been justified by faith, we have peace with God through our Lord Jesus Christ,

Ephesians 2:

8 For by grace you **have been saved** through faith, and that not of yourselves; it is the gift of God.

John 3:

16 For God so loved the world that He gave His only begotten son, that whosoever believes in Him shall not perish, but have everlasting life.

Once justified, we are promised eternal life and given the indwelling of the Holy Spirit to secure that promise.

Ephesians 4:

30 And grieve not the holy Spirit of God, whereby ye are sealed unto the day of redemption.

Glorification

Through glorification, when we receive our glorified bodies and are allowed into the presence of the Father, we **will be saved** forever from the very presence of sin.

Romans 6:

23 For all have sinned and fall short of the GLORY (Glorification) of GOD.

The Father promised, that by accepting the Son as Savior, we will break free from the sin of this life and be able to live forever in His presence. Glorification is the fulfillment of that promise.

Romans 5:

1 Therefore, having been justified by faith, we have peace with God through our Lord Jesus Christ,

2 through whom also we have access by faith into this grace in which we stand, and rejoice in hope of the glory of God.

...

8 But God demonstrates His own love toward us, in that while we were still sinners, Christ died for us.

9 Much more then, having now been justified by His blood, we shall be saved from wrath through Him.

10 For if when we were enemies we were reconciled to God through the death of His Son, much more, having been reconciled, we shall be saved by His life.

Glorification (being welcomed into the Glory of God) is the ultimate salvation and can only occur if we have accepted and acknowledged justification by the Son. We **have been** Justified by the Son and **will be** Glorified by the Father.

Sanctification
Through sanctification we are saved daily from the power of sin.

1 Corinthians 1:
18 For the message of the cross is foolishness to those who are perishing, but to us who are being saved it is the power of God.

Once justified, God could immediately call us to be in heaven, however, God leaves us here to lead others to Him. That is why we are given the indwelling of the Holy Spirit.

The Holy Spirit beckons us to accept salvation. Once justified, He lives within us to help us become more like Christ and give us the ability and power to overcome sin in our daily lives. Our sanctification by the Holy Spirit saves us from the power of sin.

We are all susceptible to sin. Paul called himself the "chief of sinners". As Christians (those who have been justified), Satan and his minions attack us constantly to destroy our witness. All who do not have the Holy Spirit are slaves to sin, but we are constantly **being saved** from sins power over us.

How do we receive salvation?
Salvation is simple as A, B, C.:

A) Acknowledge you need help.
Let's say you are on a surfboard and paddle way out, hoping to catch that really big and special wave. The wind picks up and turns from off-shore. You begin to realize that the current has also changed and is slowly dragging you further out.

No problem. You just lay down on the board and start paddling back. Paddling against wind and current is tough, but you are in great health and good shape so you increase your efforts. You make good headway, but at some point, even the best athletes wear out. As you stop to rest a minute, you just get pushed further out. As soon as you can, you get back after it.

This pattern will continue until you reach the realization that you cannot make it on your own. It is likely that you will struggle on your own until you reach the point of pending death. At that point you have to humble yourself and flag down a boat or jet ski or signal for help from the lifeguard (or anyone for that matter).

In this world, we are in an ocean of life filled with sin. Satan's objective is to keep us focused on our fun and ourselves, in constant pursuit of the next big wave, to make us content and happy. He constantly lures us into deeper water until we get caught up in the current of life. We are slowly drawn further and further from the Father and eventually we do not even acknowledge God in our life.

We will continue to do the best we can on our own, but we will not make progress until we acknowledge we need help. If we never ask for help, then we WILL ultimately drown in our sin.

Acknowledge to the Father that you cannot do it on your own, that you understand that the path you are on is drawing you out over your head; then call out to Jesus to be your savior.

Acts 2:21; Romans 10:13, 1 Cor 1:12 (and seventeen other scriptures in the Bible) say that if we call upon the name of the Lord, we WILL be saved.

NOTE: Just saying a prayer (like "Please God, save me") WILL NOT save you.

If that is all you have done in your life, self-examination is recommended.

The phrase "call upon" is more than just a cry for help. We are instructed to "repent" of our sinful ways (to make a committed effort to stay out of the situations that put us in jeopardy) and follow Him in obedience.

You can call on a lifeguard to come save you, but if you do not follow their instructions (like get in the boat), then you will still drown. Even after being pulled to shore and instructed not to go back out, if you go right back out where you came from, well … !

If you truly realized the dire situation you were in, then you will have the base desire to NOT do it again. (If you get burned reaching into a fire, then you will find every way possible to NOT reach back into the fire.)

B) Believe that Jesus shed His blood to save you.
The Son (in the form of Jesus Christ while on Earth) shed His blood as an atonement for your sin.

In Genesis 3, God sacrificed innocent animals to make coverings for Adam and Eve after they sinned. From that point on, animal sacrifice was used as the atonement for sin.

Romans 3:23 says that we ALL have sinned and fall short of the Glory of God.

Hebrews 9:22 says that without the shedding of blood there can be NO forgiveness of sin.

Through time, many people were going through the motion of sacrifice, but not repenting of sin in their heart. Animals were being sacrificed for nothing.

2 Corinthians 5:21 says that Jesus, who knew no sin, took on all the sins of man and was sacrificed on our behalf. Jesus was sacrificed for our sins.

Hebrews 10 establishes that Jesus gave Himself as the final sacrifice.

Jesus, the Lamb of God: born in a manger, wrapped in swaddling (cloth to dry new-born lambs) and visited by Levitical shepherds (who had been watching over the sacrificial lambs for the Temple in the Shepherd's Field near Bethlehem); was led as a sheep to the slaughter and died on Calvary.

No longer do we kill animals to atone for our sin, we can now look to Jesus who shed His blood for us.

1) Acknowledge to the Father that you are a sinner and Ask for His forgiveness.

2) Thank Jesus for dying on the cross and shedding His blood as punishment for your sins. Ask Him to become the Lord of your life, then give your life to Him. It is no longer yours. Jesus paid your debt.

3) Thank both Jesus and the Father for your salvation and welcome the Holy Spirit into your life to guide and empower you to live as Jesus has instructed.

C) Confess your Salvation

Matthew 10:32 says that whoever will confess Jesus before man, He will confess them before the Father.

When a person is saved from a fire or from drowning, it is almost impossible to keep them from telling about it to everyone that will listen. The same thing will happen when you truly realize that you are saved from eternal separation from God and will receive eternal life.

The Holy Spirit, now living in you, will compel you to tell others. As His primary job is to bear witness to Jesus Christ as Savior, He will do so through you.

If you are sincere in your asking to be saved, then it is done!

Contact your pastor, church staff or a teacher and they can help get you started in your new walk with Christ. If they are unavailable, or you have any questions, feel free to contact me. Bill Scherzer – Bill@OurTriuneGod. com and I will gladly discuss it with you.

Can we lose our salvation?

The answer is No, Yes and No. (You say, "WHAT????")

Justification and Glorification are promised by God.

John 3

16 For God so loved the world that He gave His only begotten son, so that whosoever believes in Him shall not perish, but have eternal life.

1 John 5:

11 And this is the record, that God hath given to us eternal life, and this life is in his Son.

12 He that hath the Son hath life; and he that hath not the Son of God hath not life.

13 These things have I written unto you that believe on the name of the Son of God; that ye may KNOW that ye have eternal life, and that ye may believe on the name of the Son of God.

Because we were justified by Christ paying our penalty, we have the promise of eternal life; and God WILL NOT break His promise.

Ephesians 4:

30 And grieve not the Holy Spirit of God, whereby ye are sealed unto the day of redemption.

When we accepted Christ as Savior, we are given the Holy Spirit as a seal (an agreement that cannot be broken – ie. a notary seal on a contract) unto the Day of Redemption (when the Father takes us into His presence through the blood Christ shed for us.) The Holy Spirit, as promised by the Father, will dwell in us until we are redeemed by Him.

Again, God cannot and will not break promises. Jesus cannot "un-die" on the cross and the Father will not take back the Holy Spirit until we are standing in His presence.

Sanctification, being saved daily by the Holy Spirit, CAN be lost. Any time we quench the Spirit we lose the Spirit's protection over the power of sin. Potentially, we can live so far in sin that we become Spiritually dead.

Romans 8:
5 For they that are after the flesh do mind the things of the flesh; but they that are after the Spirit the things of the Spirit.

6 For to be carnally minded is death; but to be spiritually minded is life and peace.

The good news is that, even after becoming "spiritually" dead, we can be revived. Since the Holy Spirit is a gift given to us by God until the day of redemption by the Father, He is still dwelling in us; He is just quenched. Revival will renew our spirit AND activate the Holy Spirit living in us where He can continue our sanctification and saving us from the power of sin in our life.

If you have not felt the presence of the Spirit in a while, He is just waiting on you. Repent of your sins (totally reject and turn away from them) and ask the Father to forgive you. Ask, and the Holy Spirit will gladly go back to work in your life. However, it cannot happen as long as you have sin you prefer in your life over the lordship of Christ.

Isaiah 59:
1 Behold, the Lord's hand is not shortened, that it cannot save; neither his ear heavy, that it cannot hear:

2 But your iniquities have separated between you and your God, and your sins have hid his face from you, that he will not hear.

Your sin can quench the Holy Spirit and temporarily sever your communication to the Father and Son.

Though, being in a carnal state and spiritually "dead", you never lose the promise of glorification paid for by the Son (justification). You can temporarily lose sanctification; however, you can be saved again from the power of sin through revival.

Psalms 51:

10 Create in me a clean heart, O God, and renew a right spirit within me.

Sin unto death

God tells us multiple times that if we accept Christ as Savior, we WILL HAVE eternal life.   God never said "but mess up and I'm taking it all back."

John 3:

16 For God so loved the world that He gave His only begotten son, so that whosoever believes in Him shall not perish, but have everlasting life.

1 John 5:

13 These things have I written unto you that believe on the name of the Son of God; that ye may know that ye have eternal life, and that ye may believe on the name of the Son of God.

Our God is such a great God! Titus 1:2 says that "God cannot lie." Sooooo... Since we all sin daily, what happens if we succumb to sin in our life? Does God break His promise? ... Of course not!

Most of the time, we endure a long drought of spiritual power which Satan uses against us. At some point, we break down, get right with God and move forward in a renewed Spirit.

Unfortunately, there are some people who get so caught up in a world of sin, that God has to step in to keep His promise.

1 John 5:

16 If any man see his brother sin a sin which is not unto death, he shall ask, and he shall give him life for them that sin not unto death.

17 There is a sin unto death: I do not say that he shall pray for it. All unrighteousness is sin: and there is a sin not unto death.

Romans 8:

12 Therefore, brethren, we are debtors, not to the flesh, to live after the flesh.

13 For if ye live after the flesh, ye shall die: but if ye through the Spirit do mortify the deeds of the body, ye shall live.

All who believe and accept the blood sacrifice of the Son (justification), WILL have everlasting life (glorification).   Once we are justified by the Son, God will call us home before we lose salvation. He will not break His promise!

If we become so caught up in sin that we are beyond being a witness for Christ, the "sin unto death" is God's way of keeping His promise in spite of ourselves.

Jesus said,

John 15:
1 I am the true vine, and my Father is the husbandman.

2 Every branch in me that beareth not fruit he taketh away: and every branch that beareth fruit, he purgeth it, that it may bring forth more fruit.

When a Christian completely stops bearing fruit, the Father takes him away (takes him home).

If you have accepted Christ as Savior and are still alive (regardless of the position you have put yourself in), then the Father IS PRUNING YOU to bear fruit. You can repent of your sin, ask for forgiveness and He will give it to you.

Psalms 51:
10 Create in me a clean heart, O God; and renew a right spirit within me.

The ONLY reason we are left on Earth after being justified is to bear fruit.

If you are alive and have no desire to bear fruit, the question you should ask is: did you ever actually accept Christ as Savior AND make Him Lord?

Abide in Christ constantly. The "world" seems to watch for Christians to slip up. Some people just watch for the opportunity to run a Christian "through the coals" in an effort to destroy them and their witness. You can't lose promises from God, but you can destroy your witness.

John 15:
6 If a man abide not in me, he is cast forth as a branch, and is withered; and men gather them, and cast them into the fire, and they are burned.

I have heard John 15:1-6 used to show that you can lose salvation from the Father. A simple examination clarified it for me (and hopefully anyone else who reads this.)

Verses 1 and 2 say that the Father "takes away" branches that no longer produce fruit. Verse 15 says that "men" will gather up branches that fail to abide in Christ and throw them in the fire.

I have not seen any place in the Bible where "men" can send people to Hell. However, in real life, the world watches in wait for Christians to sin (fail to abide in Christ). They will then rake that sinner through the coals.

Jesus was very precise. If the Lord is your Shepherd, then ...

John 10:

27 My sheep listen to My voice; I know them, and they follow Me.

28 I give them eternal life, and they will never perish. No one can snatch them out of My hand.

29 My Father who has given them to Me is greater than all. No one can snatch them out of My Father's hand.

Only your failure to accept Christ as Savior can send you to Hell, but failure of a Christian to abide in Christ can sure lead to a life of "hell on earth." As long as you are living in sin, the Spirit is quenched and you are wide open to the attacks of Satan and the world.

Always remember Titus 1:2 — That God CANNOT lie. He promised glorification to those who are justified and He WILL NOT break that promise.

SUMMARY: THREE SALVATIONS

Justification: We "have been saved" from the penalty of sin by the death of the Son on the cross.

> * Promised eternal life.
>
> * Given the Holy Spirit as a gift of God and a seal unto the Day of Redemption.

Sanctification: We "are being saved" daily from the power of sin by the Holy Spirit.

> * Indwelled by the Holy Spirit as guide, counselor and conscious for living unto Christ.
>
> * Given ability and directive to be filled with the Holy Spirit daily for spiritual warfare.

Glorification: We "will be saved" from the presence of sin on our day of redemption by the Father.

> * Receive a glorified body.
>
> * Be united with Christ at the right hand of the Father.

Three Salvations of our Triune God:

Saved by	Saved from	How	When
The Son	Penalty of sin	Justification	At the cross (past)
The Spirit	Power of sin	Sanctification	When given control (present)
The Father	Presence of sin	Glorification	Day of Redemption (future)

THREE SPIRITUAL GIFTS?

When we get saved, we are given spiritual gifts. These gifts are God given and should not be confused with talents that we can learn and develop. Spiritual gifts are beyond human ability and are for building the body of Christ, glorifying/exalting God and fighting spiritual warfare.

The more you understand spiritual gifts, the better you will be able to use them. (… and the more Satan will try to stop you – thus "spiritual warfare".) While trying to determine your active gifts, it helps to have an understanding of how the gifts work and are allocated.

When I was in my 20s, I was blessed with a gifted teacher. I attended a class she taught on spiritual gifts that has endured with me all these years. She taught that spiritual gifts fall into three categories: motivation, ministry and manifestation. However, it was not until I started studying the Trinity that I fully understood the significance of the three categories.

One day while reading Ephesians 4, it was like God put a spotlight on verses 7 and 8 with the phrase "... and He gave them gifts". It was talking about Jesus and went on to list gifts He gave. It further said that the gifts He gave were for the work of ministry.

Ephesians 4:

7 But unto every one of us is given grace according to the measure of the gift of Christ.

8 Wherefore He saith, when He ascended up on high, He led captivity captive and gave gifts unto men.

11 And He gave some, apostles; and some, prophets; and some, evangelists; and some, pastors and teachers;

12 For the perfecting of the saints, for the work of the ministry, for the edifying of the body of Christ:

After realizing that the Son gives us ministry gifts, I readily could see that the motivation gifts are from the Father and the manifestation gifts are from the Holy Spirit.

I have seen and taken several spiritual gifts tests. Most of the tests ARE accurate; however, many do not accurately interpret the results. The reason is that the person(s) applying the test often miss God's applications.

These tests bring to light the gifts that are present at the time you take the test. Your motivation gift will be present in all tests. (If you have results of tests you have taken across the years, it should help you pin-point your motivation gift.)

It is good to learn your motivation gift because it will help you understand your inner drive and base reaction in diverse situations. But it also gives you insight to where Satan will attack you the most. Every gift has weaknesses. Such as, if Satan can get a prophet caught in a lie (or presumed lie) then it lessens the people who will accept his word even when it is straight from God.

The stronger a weapon against Satan we are, the more Satan is going to fight to weaken us.

We ARE to seek spiritual gifts! We are dealing with spiritual warfare that cannot be fought without them. However, you truly need to study what you seek. Carrying a rifle onto a battlefield is definitely good, but if you have never learned how to load it, what bullets to use, how the safety works, etc. you might as well not even have it with you.

A carpenter and I can use the exact same hammer to drive three nails. He will do it with three hits. It will take me eight to ten. The difference is that he "knows" the tool.

Learn your spiritual gifts and "learn" to use them.

Let's look at just one of the manifestation gifts: the gift of healing. I have had the honor to be in the presence of spiritual healings. God worked in different ways and purpose with each.

There is no biblical process to induce God to heal - sometimes just laying on of hands will work, sometimes anointing is needed, sometimes prayer (individually or corporately), sometimes prayer AND fasting.

To study healing, look at Jesus. He rarely healed the same way. Many He healed just laying on His hands and some, He casted out demons. One lady just touched His garment (faith). He told a soldier to go home that his faith had healed his child. He told a blind man to wash in the pool of Siloam (obedience). He forgave the sins of the man lowered through the ceiling.

He put mud in the eyes of one man. He healed the man at the gate as a witness to His purpose, etc.

Since we are not God, we do not have the insight as to what is the purpose or process of the healing. We HAVE to follow guidance of the Holy Spirit. Just do as the Holy Spirit instructs you.

Don't let Satan get you down if you don't see immediate healing, just keep going. (Mark 8:22-26 > Jesus touched the man twice to completely heal his sight.) Healing is not always immediate.

I have an x-ray of a friend taken in the ER showing a clear break in her leg that was going to need at least three screws. Since she was on blood thinners for another issue, they had to keep her in the hospital three days while her blood got right. Our prayer team started the night of the break, and when the doctors felt she could handle the procedure, they x-rayed again to confirm screw positions and discovered a complete healing. They were amazed and she walked out of the hospital! PTL

One October, smoke came up from fires in Mexico and my younger daughter (with dextrocardia – five open heart surgeries at the time) went into arrhythmia (heart beating well into life-threatening range.) They had to give her a shot to stop her heart and restart it to get it down to safe levels. They determined she had enough damage that another open-heart surgery was required.

Needless to say, the prayers started.

She had to go in weekly for testing and monitoring. Five months later, they determined the damage still needed surgery and that she was strong enough to handle it. They scheduled her for a special team of doctors (familiar with dextrocardia) and brought her into the hospital the day prior for preparatory tests. The doctors were in awe. After five months of tests showing damage, she was clear and stable. They expressed their befuddlement! Their words, "... not only do we not have to operate, we don't even need to see her again for six months." I just said, "Isn't God good?" They said they didn't have any other answer and smiled.

The point is, God could have healed her when we first asked, but He was exalted and was revealed to all the doctors and medical staff that had been working with her by waiting the five months.

We do not know God's timing in any situation.

Seek daily to be filled with the Holy Spirit, then follow His guidance. Walking in the Spirit puts us in the best position to be used by the Spirit.

The Gifts

Motivation, Ministry and Manifestation

Motivation:

Our motivation gift is to direct us to our work within the church – the body of Christ.

Your motivation gift was given to you by the Father as part of the new creation you become when you accept Christ as your Savior. This establishes you as YOUR part of the body of Christ and joint heir with Him.

Romans 12:

3 For I say, through the grace given unto me, to every man that is among you, not to think of himself more highly than he ought to think; but to think soberly, according as God hath dealt to every man the measure of faith.

4 For as we have many members in one body, and all members have not the same office:

5 So we, being many, are one body in Christ, and every one members one of another.

6a Having then gifts differing according to the grace that is given to us,

We receive our motivation gift the moment the we accept Christ as our Savior. This gift defines our part in the body and is the underlying source of our actions in fulfilling our purpose in the church – our "motivation".

To me, v.4 clearly indicates that, as pertaining to the body, every person is an individual part - that one person is not an arm, a leg and a mouth all rolled into one.

All seven motivation gifts (prophecy, serving, exhortation, giving, teaching, administration and mercy) are needed for a church to run at maximum efficiency. Seven people, each with one of the gifts, will accomplish much more than two or three people having to split time doing their job and the jobs of the missing gifts.

Which functions best, a body with all its parts or a body missing a leg, an arm, the mouth (mute), the ears (deaf), etc.?

A body missing parts is handicapped. A handicapped body CAN still succeed, but the workload is much harder for that body. A deaf or mute person can use their hands to talk, but while the hands are needed to talk, they can't be carrying a load.

Just because you may have multiple gifts at work at any point in time, that does not make you "parts" of the body. YOUR part of the body is a full-time gift - your Motivation gift.

Ministry:

Our ministry gifts are given to us to complete ongoing, and often ever-changing, assignments.

Ephesians 4:

7 But unto every one of us is given grace according to the measure of the gift of Christ.

8 Wherefore He saith, when He ascended up on high, He led captivity captive and gave gifts unto men.

11 And He gave some, apostles; and some, prophets; and some, evangelists; and some, pastors and teachers;

12 For the perfecting of the saints, for the work of the ministry, for the edifying of the body of Christ:

Ministry gifts are given to us by the Son to accomplish specific missions. It could be long term, as for developing a ministry within the church, or possibly short term to fill an immediate need.

I have had times when I can feel a person who is down and like out of the blue I get a word from God that exhorts them. I have met people (hopefully you too) that have experienced that moment of "knowing" they have lifted someone up by sharing something, then have to say to themselves "Wow, where did that come from?".

The key about ministry gifts is that as soon as the mission Jesus has assigned to you is completed, keep your eyes open for your next mission. You will find that the Son provides ministry gifts in line with the ministry need He desires you to fulfill.

Manifestation:

Manifestation gifts are often identified as tools and weapons of spiritual warfare. Where motivation and ministry gifts empower an individual to build the body of the church, manifestation gifts empower an individual to stand and work against the spirits trying to destroy the body while at the same time present the power of God to the body for His glory.

1 Corinthians 12:

7 To each is given the manifestation of the Spirit for the common good.

8 For to one is given through the Spirit the utterance of wisdom, and to another the utterance of knowledge according to the same Spirit,

9 to another faith by the same Spirit, to another gifts of healing by the one Spirit,

10 to another the working of miracles, to another prophecy, to another the ability to distinguish between spirits, to another various kinds of tongues, to another the interpretation of tongues.

11 All these are empowered by one and the same Spirit, who apportions to each one individually as he wills.

Manifestation gifts are manifested as the Holy Spirit directs. They are God driven and God implemented - we are simply the conduit being used. The Holy Spirit is directed to our assignments and knows the tools we need to complete them. He equips us with the gifts needed - as needed.

*** BE FILLED DAILY ***

The Holy Spirit empowers "as He wills", but is unable if we have Him quenched. We all tend to sin daily. It is in our nature. Paul called himself the "chief of sinners" … and he wrote a lot of the New Testament.

"When" we sin (even a passive thought of pride, lust or ambition), it is all a matter of how we handle it. Best case, we just quickly acknowledge it, tell God we're sorry and move on.

The problems come when we dwell on it. For example: Someone says something to us or cuts us off in traffic, etc. We respond in anger and our mind starts to focus on how "we" have been offended. A sin of pride comes out.

The more time we spend focusing on how we have been offended, the more of a field-day Satan has. Sometimes we can let it affect our whole day and potentially all those around us.

The sad part is that when we are dwelling in our sin, the Holy Spirit is hindered. It is not until we realize that we have let "self" override the Spirit that we can let the Spirit step forward and take care of things for us.

Anytime self is in control, the Spirit is quenched.

Asking the Holy Spirit daily to take charge of your day will allow Him to shorten the time you react to and dwell in your sins. Having a Spirit-filled life is simply a matter of keeping yourself available for the Holy Spirit to use you "as He wills".

SUMMARY: THREE SPIRITUAL GIFTS

Our Motivation gift is given by the Father and establishes our part of the body of Christ.

Our Ministerial gifts are given by the Son to complete the work He wants us to do.

Our Manifestation gifts are given by the Holy Spirit to equip us for spiritual warfare and to strengthen/support the body.

VISUAL SUMMARY

Below is an overview of how God being the Trinity affects our Christian walk.

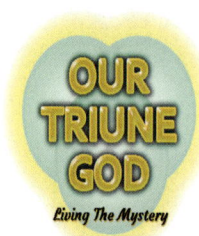

	FATHER	SON	HOLY SPIRIT
Location	In Heaven	Right hand of the Father	Everywhere
Primary Attribute	Omniscient (knows everything)	Omnipotent (created everything)	Omnipresent (is everywhere)
Salvation	Glorification:	Justification:	Sanctification:
Saved from:	Presence of sin	Penalty of sin	Power of sin
When saved:	Day of Redemption (future)	Acknowledgement and acceptance of the cruxifiction of Christ as payment for our sin. (past)	When given control. (present)
Spiritual Sin	Lust of the eyes	Lust of the flesh	Pride of life
Spiritual Gifts	Motivation:	Ministry:	Manifestation:
Purpose:	Our part in the body of Christ	Fulfilling ministry	Spiritual warfare
When received:	Acceptance of Christ as Savior	As needed	Indwelling of Holy Spirit
Duration:	Perminant	Completion of ministry	Always available (toolkit/arsenal)

Living the Mystery

Knowing the mystery does not match "living" the mystery. Action is superior to knowledge.

You now have "another" perspective to add to your learning. Hopefully, the Holy Spirit has used part of mine to build up the work you are doing already or to set you in motion for the work God has for you to accomplish.

Knowing and seeing the Trinity at work in all areas of the Christian walk has been, and still is, a great joy for me. Use anything you have gained from this book, whether written by me or via revelation of the Holy Spirit, to empower your daily walk.

To many people, "how" electricity works is a mystery to them, yet they don't walk around in the dark. They rely on people who have learned the mystery to add to their lives.

There are many people that do not know (or even want to know) God. Who God is and how God works is a mystery to them, but the goodness of God stills falls on the just and the unjust.

To electricians and all who study the mystery of electricity, they live in the world with confidence that they will never be locked into darkness. The same is with people who study God and His mysteries. Knowing God puts you in position to "see" God at work in areas that appear dark to most. You can live in confidence in this world knowing God.

Many people rely on those who study God to help them live in this world.

The Holy Spirit reveals the "Word of God" as we are able to digest and use what we learn.

Use what God has given you. "Live" in the mystery and help others along the way.

ABOUT THE AUTHOR

Computer tech by trade and Sunday School teacher when needed; my life is the product of many parts brought together as much by God's design as it was circumstance.

When I was about 5 or 6 and just learning to read, I picked up a Bible that was on my grandmother's dresser and was looking through it. A verse popped out to me because it was the only one I knew all the words:

"Let your light so shine before men that they may see your good work and glorify our Father which is in heaven. Matthew 5:16"

I took the Bible and read it to my mom, dad and grandmother and they explained what it meant. It was the first verse I memorized and it has been an influence my whole life.

Saved at the age of 8 during a Vacation Bible School, I haven't lived a perfect life, but I have been protected. As a child, I leaned on this simple verse most of the time:

"What times I'm afraid I will trust in Thee. Psalms 56:3"

While in the ninth grade, during Training Union one Sunday, I made a commitment to never smoke or drink; and with God's help and guidance, I have kept that vow. That same year, I wrote a poem that stayed on the wall over my bed for many years that helped keep me on track:

When each day has come to pass,
I lay my head to rest,
And pray to God that I can say,
In all I gave my best.

I grew up in Scouting and became an Eagle, then later a Scoutmaster and District Commissioner. I learned and lived duty to God and Country, to others and to self.

In the tenth grade, our school got its first computer and my math teacher said that anything we could program the computer do, we would not have to do as homework. That was like saying "sick'm" to a bulldog for me and launched my life in computers. As a senior, I went to a career development high school and studied programming, then worked in computer operations to pay for college.

In 1983, I started Rheagl Services Company helping companies and individuals with business development. Still today, I use a mantra of:

"Doing my best to help others be their best."

As a single adult, I was active with the singles at my church and started teaching a single's Sunday School class. When I met my wife, we worked in the Single's department for several years and raised two great daughters.

I could write a whole book trying to just highlight my life and how it has made me who I am. I have expanded experience in the music business, both my daughters have dextrocardia, I have a bucket list item to catch a fish in every state park in Texas; and a lot more.

I haven't had an affluent life, but I have had the abundant life that God promises to those who put Him first. I am now at the point of

"To whom much is given, much is required."

Thus, I have written this book to help others know God better and help them live a more fulfilling life.

William O. Scherzer, III

OurTriuneGod.com